THE LIVING RAIN FOREST

An Animal Alphabet

PAUL KRATTER

 Charlesbridge

For my biggest supporter, Tia, and my two boys, Joel and Marshall

Thank you:
The Oakland Zoo; San Francisco Zoo; San Diego Zoo; Los Angeles Zoo;
California Academy of Sciences; Museum of Vertebrate Zoology,
University of California, Berkeley; and especially my brother, Andy Kratter,
collection manager in ornithology, Florida Museum of Natural History
—P. K.

Animal lengths include entire body unless otherwise noted. Birds are measured from the end of the beak to the end of the tail. Butterflies are measured by wingspan.

Published by Charlesbridge
85 Main Street
Watertown, MA 02472
(617) 926-0329
www.charlesbridge.com

Library of Congress Cataloging-in-Publication Data
Kratter, Paul.
The living rain forest : an animal alphabet / Paul Kratter.
p. cm.
Summary: Introduces twenty-six rain forest animals from A to Z,
providing the name, favorite foods, and unique characteristics of each.
ISBN 978-1-58089-392-3 (reinforced for library use)
ISBN 978-1-58089-393-0 (softcover)
1. Rain forest animals—Juvenile literature. 2. Rain forests—Juvenile literature.
3. English language—Alphabet—Juvenile literature. 4. Alphabet books. I. Title.
QL112.K73 2010
578.734–dc22   2009048586

Printed in Singapore
(hc) 10 9 8 7 6 5 4 3 2 1
(sc) 10 9 8 7 6 5 4 3 2 1

Illustrations done in acrylics and watercolors on Strathmore watercolor board
Display type set in Opti Caslon Antique; text type set in New Baskerville and Tekton
Color separations by ArtScans Studio, Inc., Manhattan Beach, California
Printed and bound April 2010 by Imago in Singapore
Production supervision by Brian G. Walker
Designed by Paul Kratter and Diane M. Earley

Introduction

Rain forests cover only six percent of the earth's land, yet contain more than half its animal and plant species. Unfortunately this unique habitat is threatened by deforestation, global warming, and overhunting. In the past two hundred years we have lost more than half the world's rain forests.

This book features just a few of the millions of species of animals found only in tropical rain forests. Each animal has special adaptations to help it live in its environment. But like the rain forests they inhabit, all these creatures face extinction.

The Living Rain Forest teaches people about the rare, diverse, and beautiful animal life of the rain forest. If we grow to appreciate our rain forests, we can preserve them before it's too late.

A anteater

GIANT ANTEATER (Myrmecophaga tridactyla)
Body 3–4 feet, tail 2–4 feet

The giant anteater is toothless. It uses its long snout to locate ant nests or termite mounds. The anteater uses its powerful claws to tear open a mound and then lick up its meal with a long, sticky tongue.

B butterfly

MORPHO BUTTERFLY (Morpho menelaus)
Wingspan 3.5–4.5 inches

The morpho butterfly sips the nectar of flowers through its proboscis. The brown undersides of its wings are good camouflage in the rain forest. As it flies, the butterfly seems to appear and then disappear against the background, making it hard to catch.

Camouflage: *A pattern or disguise to hide something. Coloring or covering that allows animals to blend in with or hide in their surroundings.*

Proboscis: *A tubular projection from the mouth of an insect used for sucking.*

C chameleon

PARSON'S CHAMELEON (Chamaeleo parsonii)

Length 29–35 inches

The Parson's chameleon has a long, sticky tongue that it uses to catch insects to eat. It changes colors if scared or to match its surroundings.

D dolphin

AMAZON RIVER DOLPHIN (Inia geoffrensis)

Length 6.5–8.5 feet

The Amazon river dolphin has very small eyes. It uses echolocation to locate its prey swimming in murky water. It also pokes its head in the muddy river bottom to find crabs, fish, and turtles to eat.

Echolocation: *A way to locate an object using sound waves.*

E eagle

HARPY EAGLE (Harpia harpyja)
Length 34–36 inches

The harpy eagle is armed with powerful feet, huge talons, and a strong beak. It swoops through the treetops hunting a variety of animals including monkeys, opossums, sloths, and snakes.

Talons: *Claws of a bird.*

F frog

DART POISON FROG (Dendrobates azureus)

Length 1.5 inches

The dart poison frog's bright colors warn other animals that its skin is toxic. This tiny amphibian eats ants, termites, and other insects.

Amphibian: *Cold-blooded animal that has a backbone. Amphibians live in water and breathe with gills when young, but develop lungs and live on land as adults.*
Toxic: *Poisonous.*

G gorilla

MOUNTAIN GORILLA (Gorilla beringei beringei)
Length 4.5–6.5 feet

The mountain gorilla is the largest, and one of the
rarest, primates. It eats a wide variety of plants, including
bamboo, wild celery, roots, fruit, soft bark, and fungi.

Fungi: Mushroom-type organisms that feed on decaying or dead material.

Primates: Mammals including humans, apes, monkeys, and lemurs. Primates
have large brains, forward-facing eyes, and five digits on each hand and foot.

H honeycreeper

HAWAIIAN HONEYCREEPER (Vestiaria coccinea)

Length 6 inches

The Hawaiian honeycreeper is found only on the islands of Hawaii. Its curved bill and brushlike tongue help it gather nectar from flowers.

Nectar: *The sugary liquid of a plant that attracts insects, birds, and bats to pollinate.*

I iguana

GREEN IGUANA (Iguana iguana)

Length 4–6 feet

The green iguana is mainly arboreal, but it's also a good swimmer. The female lays up to seventy eggs in a nest buried in the ground.

Arboreal: *Lives in or spends a good deal of time in trees.*

 jaguar

JAGUAR (Panthera onca)
Body 3.5–6.5 feet, tail 18–30 inches

The powerful jaguar likes to swim and is a good tree climber. It hunts at night for a wide range of prey including deer, reptiles, and aquatic animals.

Aquatic: *Living or growing in water.*

K katydid

LEAF KATYDID (Mimetica incisa)

Length 1–2.5 inches

The leaf katydid lies motionless during the day to hide from predators. It becomes active at night, feeding on leaves, shoots, and flowers.

Predator: *An animal that hunts other animals for food.*

 lemur

BLACK AND WHITE RUFFED LEMUR
(*Varecia variegata variegata*)
Body 22 inches, tail 3.5–4 feet

The black and white ruffed lemur is a noisy primate.
It will grunt and even roar when alarmed. Fruit, nectar,
seeds, and leaves make up its diet.

M macaw

BLUE AND YELLOW MACAW (Ara ararauna)

Length 35 inches

The blue and yellow macaw uses its large hooked beak for eating fruit and for climbing in the canopy. This social bird is usually found in pairs and can be seen in flocks of up to thirty birds.

Canopy: Sheltered area under the treetops.

N night monkey

NIGHT MONKEY (Aotus trivirgatus)
Body 12–16 inches, tail 11.5–17.5 inches

The night monkey is nocturnal and has huge eyes that help it see in the dark. It makes a soft hooting noise like an owl. The night monkey feeds on fruit, flowers, leaves, and insects.

Nocturnal: *Active at night.*

O okapi

OKAPI (Okapia johnstoni)
Length 6.5–7.5 feet

The okapi feeds on leaves by stripping them from branches with its long prehensile tongue. This close relative of the giraffe is shy and rarely seen.

Prehensile: *Adapted for grabbing, especially by wrapping around.*

P piranha

RED-BELLIED PIRANHA (Pygocentrus nattereri)

Length 6–8 inches

The red-bellied piranha lives in fresh water and hunts in schools. It will attack any animal splashing in the water. A piranha darts in and bites off small pieces of flesh with its sharp teeth.

School: *A group of the same kind of fish.*

quetzal

RESPLENDENT QUETZAL
(Pharomachrus mocinno)

Body 14 inches, tail 25 inches

The resplendent quetzal feeds mainly on fruit but will also eat small lizards and insects. The male attracts a female by swooping down from the canopy and letting the long covert feathers in his tail flow through the air.

Resplendent: *Shining brightly.*
Covert feathers: *Feathers covering the quills of a bird's wings and tail.*

R rhinoceros

SUMATRAN RHINOCEROS (*Dicerorhinus sumatrensis*)

Length 8.5–10 feet

The shy Sumatran rhinoceros keeps itself cool and free of biting insects by rolling in mud. It feeds at night on vegetation near water. It is the smallest and hairiest kind of rhinoceros.

S sloth

THREE-TOED SLOTH
(Bradypus infuscatus)

Length 18–20 inches

The three-toed sloth is slow-moving. It spends the day hanging upside down feeding on leaves. Greenish algae growing on its fur help hide the sloth from predators.

Algae: *Small plants that grow in water.*

T toucan

KEEL-BILLED TOUCAN
(Ramphastos sulfuratus)

Length 20 inches

The keel-billed toucan's bill is lightweight and used to grab fruit, insects, and even the eggs of other birds. Both parents care for their young in a nest made in a hollow tree.

Uakari

RED UAKARI (Cacajao calvus rubicundus)

Body 15–22.5 inches, tail 5.5–7.5 inches

The red uakari is a short-tailed monkey. Its strong jaws help it eat fruit with hard outer shells that other monkeys can't eat. The uakari lives in a large group of twenty to thirty animals.

V viper

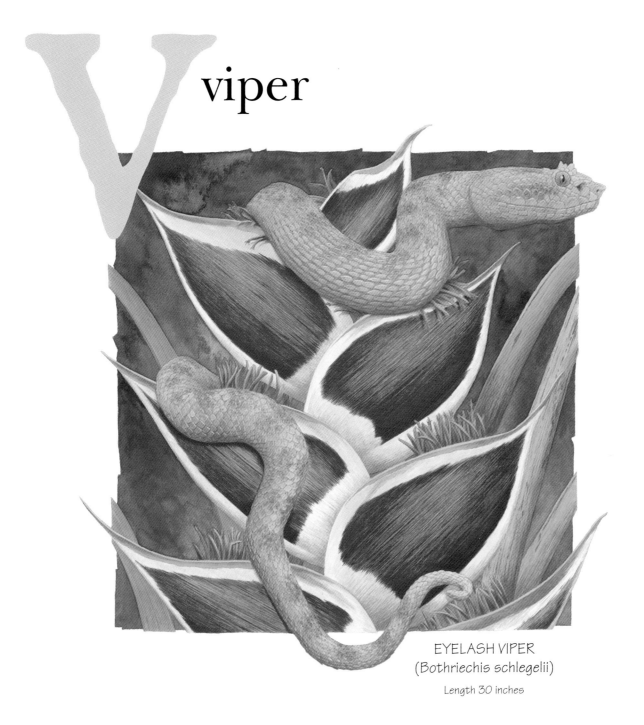

EYELASH VIPER
(Bothriechis schlegelii)

Length 30 inches

The eyelash viper will lie motionless waiting for a small bird or mammal to pass. The viper strikes quickly, using poison from its fangs to stop its prey.

W wallaby

BLACK FOREST WALLABY (Dorcopsis atrata)
Body 29–39 inches, tail 11–15 inches

The black forest wallaby is a marsupial. It gives birth to a small baby, called a joey, that develops fully in its mother's pouch. It feeds at night on many kinds of plants.

Marsupial: A mammal such as a kangaroo or opossum. The females have a pouch that serves to carry their young.

X xenops

PLAIN XENOPS (Xenops minutus)

Length 5 inches

The bill of the plain xenops is designed to peck and probe. The xenops climbs dead branches and vines looking for insects to eat.

Y yapok

YAPOK (Chironectes minimus)
Body 10–16 inches, tail 12–17 inches

The yapok is a type of opossum. This aquatic marsupial has a pouch that can be closed tightly underwater. Webbed feet help the yapok swim as it hunts for fish, frogs, and other freshwater prey.

Z zorro

ZORRO (Atelocynus microtis)
Body 28–40 inches, tail 9–13 inches

The zorro is a type of dog. It eats rodents, small mammals, and some plants. Very little is known about this rare creature.

Rodents: *Mammals with sharp teeth used for gnawing, such as mice, rats, squirrels, and beavers.*

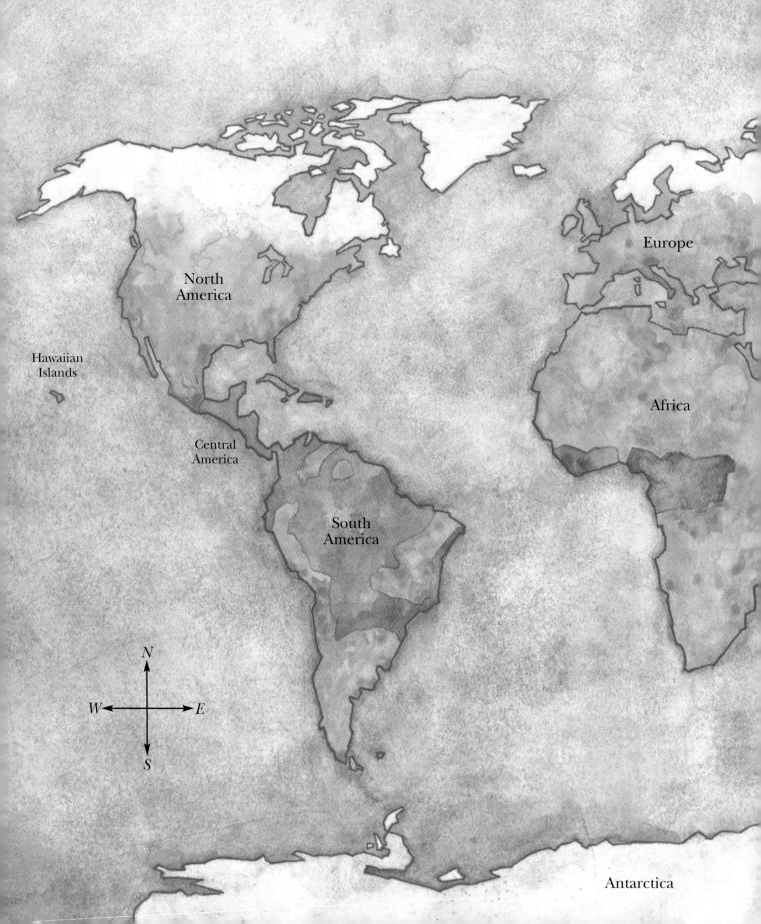

Tropical Rain Forest

Hawaiian
Islands

North
America

Central
America

South
America

Europe

Africa

N
W — E
S

Antarctica

of the World

Asia

Madagascar

Australia

Locations of Animals Found in This Book

A giant anteater—Central and South America
B morpho butterfly—South America
C Parson's chameleon—Africa
D Amazon river dolphin—South America
E harpy eagle—Central and South America
F dart poison frog—South America
G mountain gorilla—Africa
H Hawaiian honeycreeper—Hawaiian Islands
I green iguana—Central and South America
J jaguar—Central and South America
K leaf katydid—Central and South America
L black and white ruffed lemur—Madagascar
M blue and yellow macaw—South America
N night monkey—South America
O okapi—Africa
P red-bellied piranha—South America
Q resplendent quetzal—Central America
R Sumatran rhinoceros—Southeast Asia
S three-toed sloth—South America
T keel-billed toucan—Central America
U red uakari—South America
V eyelash viper—Central America
W black forest wallaby—Australia
X xenops—Central and South America
    Y yapok—Central and South America
    Z zorro—South America

Key

tropical rain forests

Emergent Layer— Tallest trees can reach 130 feet.

Canopy Layer— These trees cut off much of the sunlight to the rest of the forest. Trees measure 65 feet high or more.

Mid Layer— Trees measure 15 to 65 feet.

Shrub Layer— Vegetation here is sparse compared to canopy. Trees and plants grow to 15 feet.

Ground Layer— Fungi, ferns, herbs, and small seedlings are found here.

Resources

Organizations:

Rainforest Action Network
221 Pine Street, 5th Floor
San Francisco, CA 94104
(415) 398-4404
www.ran.org

The Rainforest Alliance
665 Broadway, Suite 500
New York, NY 10012
(212) 677-1900
www.rainforest-alliance.org

Books:

Berger, Melvin, and Gilda Berger. *Does It Always Rain in the Rain Forest?: Questions and Answers About Tropical Rain Forests* (Scholastic Question and Answer Series). New York: Scholastic Reference, 2002.

Cherry, Lynne. *The Great Kapok Tree: A Tale of the Amazon Rain Forest.* San Diego, CA: Harcourt, Inc.; Voyager Books edition, 2000.

Cheshire, Gerard. *The Tropical Rainforest* (Nature Unfolds). New York: Crabtree Publishing Company, 2001.

Collard, Sneed B., III. *The Forest in the Clouds.* Watertown, MA: Charlesbridge, 2000.

Greenaway, Theresa. *Jungle* (Eyewitness Books). New York: DK Publishing, 2009.

Wilkes, Angela. *Rain Forest* (Question Time: Explore and Discover). New York: Kingfisher, 2002.

Willow, Diane. *At Home in the Rain Forest.* Watertown, MA: Charlesbridge, 1991.